# Honouring the Holy Spirit

PAUL MOULD

# Honouring the Holy Spirit

Copyright © 2021 PAUL MOULD

All rights reserved.

ISBN: 9798479238550

Cover image: Cullan Smith, unsplash.com

# Honouring the Holy Spirit

## CONTENTS

Acknowledgments

| | | |
|---|---|---|
| 1 | Why Should We Honour the Spirit? | Pg 1 |
| 2 | Honouring the Spirit: The Personal Connection | Pg 6 |
| 3 | Honouring the Spirit: The Corporate Connection | Pg 18 |
| 4 | Honouring the Spirit: The Revival Connection | Pg 24 |
| | Footnotes | Pg 30 |
| | Bible Quotations | Pg 33 |
| | About the Author | Pg 34 |

# Honouring the Holy Spirit

## ACKNOWLEDGMENTS

My sincere thanks go to all those individuals who have helped me to encounter and learn about the Holy Spirit down the years, especially in 1994. I give special thanks to Jacquie and Terry from my former cell group, who were really receptive to my teaching about honouring the Holy Spirit - your encouragement meant so much. Thanks especially to my wife for your support, patience and proof-reading. Finally, I am grateful for the sermons of C. H. Spurgeon for articulating what was in my heart but couldn't find the words to express.

**Glory be to the Father,**

**And to the Son,**

**And to the Holy Spirit**

# Honouring the Holy Spirit

## 1 WHY SHOULD WE HONOUR THE SPIRIT?

On the evening before his crucifixion, Jesus promised his disciples to send another Comforter (John 14:16, KJV). The word 'another' - *allos* (original Greek) means another of the same kind. He is like Jesus was to his disciples: Teacher, Guide, Encourager...He is the One with us now. Jesus is seated at the right hand of the Father but he has not left us as orphans (John 14:18). He has sent the Spirit to be with us for ever. The introductory verses of the book of Acts (Acts 1:1-5) make it clear that the work that Jesus began is continued by the Holy Spirit. We are now living in the Age of the Spirit. Just as Jesus deserves honour, the Spirit of Jesus deserves to be honoured among us. Honouring the Spirit doesn't somehow mean we will neglect the Person of Jesus, because the Spirit brings glory to Jesus. Honouring the Holy Spirit will not result in less glory going to Jesus but more! To honour the Spirit means to value, appreciate, thank and praise Him; to hold Him in high esteem. We worship Him because He's worthy of it. It is right and fitting to praise the Holy Spirit, just as it is right and fitting to praise the Father and Son.

Evangelist John Van Gelderen makes these observations: "Jesus said of the Spirit, 'He shall glorify me' (John 16:14). But He never said we are not to glorify the Spirit. This is a leap some people make that is not in the text. Since the Spirit reveals the Son, it follows that we should honour the Spirit in order to honour the Son." If we sincerely desire to honour the Son, we must also honour the Spirit. "When the Scripture says 'Honor God' but does not specify which person of the Godhead, does it not include Father, Son, and Spirit? The Spirit should be glorified as God along with the Father and the Son. This is not a matter of getting out of balance, but getting back into balance."[1]

Some have also pointed out that there are no recorded prayers to the Holy Spirit in the New Testament; in contrast, there are prayers directed to the Father and to Jesus. Therefore, it is suggested that it is wrong to pray to the Holy Spirit. However, this view is misguided because there are plenty of occasions in the Book of Acts where the Spirit speaks to and directs the disciples (e.g. 8:29, 16:6-7, 20:23). We can only conclude there was a two-way conversation going on. And if prayer is simply defined as conversing with God, then there is plenty of evidence for praying to the Spirit in scripture. Again, the words "the fellowship of the Holy Spirit" (2 Cor 13:14) must imply a relationship in which we dialogue with Him.

The great danger in not honouring and worshipping the Spirit is that in practice we are saying that the Spirit is lesser than the Father and Son. It doesn't matter that we say we believe in the Trinity, one God in three persons - if we fail to give due worship to the Holy Spirit we are actually practicing heresy; we are treating the Holy Spirit as a second-tier member of the Trinity. That may sound harsh but in the fourth century there was a major Christian sect that believed the Spirit to be inferior to the Father and the Son. The need to defend the truth of the Spirit's divinity played a big part in early church councils that put together the Nicene Creed, which says that the Spirit is to be co-worshipped and co-glorified with the Father and the Son. This was made more explicit in the Athanasian Creed (5th century): "But the Godhead of the Father, of the Son, and of the Holy Ghost, is all one: the Glory equal, the Majesty co-eternal. And in this Trinity none is before, or after another: none is greater, or less than another; But the whole three Persons are co-eternal together: and co-equal. So that in all things... [the] Trinity in Unity is to be worshiped." The point I am making is this: it's no use having a *written* creed that states that the Holy Spirit is fully God if our *working* creed is that only the Father and Son are worthy of worship. We must also give time to worshipping the Holy Spirit. And if some might argue that worshipping the Spirit was not the practice in the early church, consider this doxology by Polycarp (a disciple of the apostle John, d. 155AD) "[Father] I praise Thee, I bless Thee, I glorify Thee; through our eternal High Priest in heaven, thy beloved Son Jesus Christ, by whom and with whom be glory to Thee and the Holy Spirit now and for all the ages to come. Amen."[2]

There are two other errors that have crept into the modern church that have taken honour away from the Holy Spirit. First, mainly referring to the Spirit indirectly, in such terms as "The presence of God", "The anointing", "The Fire", "The River", and so on. If overused, these terms have the effect of depersonalising the Holy Spirit. Second, an emphasis on seeking the gifts of the Spirit, rather than seeking the Spirit Himself. Some churches, for example, speak much more about prophecy than the Person of the Holy Spirit. Both these practices rob the Holy Spirit of honour that belongs to Him.

While researching for this book I have discovered great wisdom on honouring the Holy Spirit in the sermons of the famous nineteenth century preacher C.H. Spurgeon[3], and you will find a number of quotes from him in these pages. Although he was speaking over 150 years ago, his words have never been more relevant. For example:

"Dear Brothers and Sisters, honor the Spirit of God as you would honor Jesus Christ if He were present! …Do not ignore the Presence of the Holy Spirit in your soul! I beseech you…To Him pay your constant adorations. Reverence the august Guest who has been pleased to make your body His sacred abode. Love Him, obey Him, worship Him!"[4]

"We do not hesitate to say, that we owe as much to God the Holy Ghost as we do to God the Son. Indeed, it were a high sin and misdemeanour to attempt to put one person of the Divine Trinity before another. Thou, O Father, art the source of all grace, all love and mercy towards us. Thou, O Son, art the channel of thy Father's mercy, and without thee thy Father's love could never flow to us. And thou, O Spirit—thou art he who enables us to receive that divine virtue which flows from the fountainhead, the Father, through Christ the channel, and by thy means enters into our spirit, and there abides and brings forth its glorious fruit. Magnify, then, the Spirit…'praise, laud, and love his name always, for it is seemly so to do'"[5]

In the following chapters we will consider in more detail how the Holy Spirit should be honoured individually and corporately, and how honouring the Holy Spirit is a key to revival.

# Honouring the Holy Spirit

# 2 HONOURING THE SPIRIT: THE PERSONAL CONNECTION

What does it mean to honour the Holy Spirit in our individual lives? The apostle Paul tells us that "the Kingdom of God is not a matter of eating or drinking, but of righteousness, peace and joy in the Holy Spirit" (Rom 14:17). This is what the Christian life is all about. It's not about following religious rules and set patterns but living under the influence and direction of the Holy Spirit. Jesus lived a life fully yielded to and permeated with the Holy Spirit (Luke 4:18, Acts 10:38). We are saved so that we could be like Him (Rom 8:29). True Christianity is about a demonstration of the Spirit's life and power: "righteousness, peace and joy in the Holy Spirit". It should be clear that life in the Spirit is no add-on, no bolt-on, no optional extra; it's absolutely central to living how God wants us to live.

**Power for right living**

To honour the Spirit personally means to be submitted to Him in all things, following His promptings and impulses and not those of our sinful nature. God's purpose is *"that the righteousness of the law might be fulfilled in us, who walk not after the flesh, but after the Spirit (Rom 8:4, KJV).* "That the righteousness of the law - the holiness it required… might be fulfilled in us, who walk not after the flesh, but after the Spirit - Who are guided in all our thoughts, words, and actions, not by corrupt nature, but by the Spirit of God."[6]

The command "Be filled with the Holy Spirit" (Eph 5:17) has been described as the "ultimate imperative"[7]. I would indeed agree that "Be filled with the Spirit" is the greatest command given to believers, because by obeying this one command we are enabled to fulfil all others.

"Since we live by the Spirit, let us keep in step with the Spirit" (Gal 5:25). We have received the life of the Spirit (He lives in us) but it's our responsibility to be directed and controlled by the Spirit. We do this by developing a love relationship with Him. Our life abounding with His; our weakness combined with His Almighty strength. We are called to walk in step with Him, as a company of soldiers marching in rank. That is, we should "follow the Spirit's leading in every area of our lives" (Gal 5:25, NLT). We should keep in step with Him, not running ahead of Him, and not lagging behind. The Holy Spirit doesn't move according to our schedule, instead we are to seek out and respond to His schedule. He won't fit in with our timetable, we must give Him room to do what He wants to do.

We walk in the Spirit by maintaining an inner dialogue with the Spirit, through thoughts, words, impressions etc. Put more simply, we walk in the Spirit by talking with the Spirit. This is so simple, but so easily missed. We need to give time, quieten ourselves down and tune in. It's like finding a radio station using an old analogue radio. There's lots of pop, fizz, crackle, but then you find the right frequency. There is plenty of pop, fizz and crackle in this world, but we need to find the secret place and dwell there. Often He speaks through the Scriptures but in many other ways also. He can speak anytime (often unexpectedly), so we must stay in tune.


## Peace and Joy

In the Bible, the word 'peace' implies wholeness and well-being. This brings us to the heart of the gospel message. There are hints in the Old Testament concerning the nature of the Holy Spirit, but He is only fully revealed in the New. He is the One who applies Christ's work of redemption to our lives, making saints out of sinners. He is the One who brings us into intimacy with both Father and Son; He is the One we can freely give ourselves to. He is fully a person, someone, not something. Someone you can get to know. Someone you can gladly and joyfully surrender your whole life to. God is Love, His Spirit is Love. God's love is poured into our hearts by the Holy Spirit. (Rom 5:5). He is the One who delights in us, who cherishes us. Only in union with Him do we find true fulfilment, lasting peace and joy. We should desire to be saturated by, permeated by, drenched with and overflow with the Holy Spirit - not a trickle but a flood as we give over the whole of our lives to the Holy Spirit. Too often we treat being filled with the Spirit as a quick 'splash 'n' dash' but we are to be continually filled, like standing in the rain until we are wet through. We need to spend time soaking in His presence[9]. Don't rush off before He's met with you in a deep way. It's not just about receiving more of the Holy Spirit; it's also about giving more of ourselves to Him. We are made for a love union with Him.

"Be filled with the Spirit" (Eph 5:17) is not only a command, it's also an invitation. When we ask the Spirit to fill us we should also gladly surrender our lives to Him. Early Christian writers such as Augustine described the Spirit as the bond of love between the Father and Son, and their eternal embrace. When we surrender ourselves to the Spirit, we are giving ourselves to the Person who is the very essence of intimate love and fellowship. What joy, what delight, what privilege![8] We can gladly say "I am His, and He is mine" (Song 2:16).

The Holy Spirit is affectionate towards you; will you be affectionate towards Him? When the Bible says the Holy Spirit 'fell' on a group of people, the word 'fell' in the original Greek means an affectionate embrace (e.g. the same word is used in Luke 15:20 when the father embraced the lost son). Will you respond warmly, or in cold indifference? Will you return His words of affection or ignore them? The love of God He pours into your heart; will you return it to Him? God's love cannot be earned; it can only be received or rejected. Will you warmly receive his love today? To honour the Holy Spirit means to embrace a love relationship with Him. Carol Arnott (former leader of Catch the Fire church in Toronto) tells us that "He is patient, forgiving, and long-suffering. He is called the Comforter and He truly is the most wonderful friend and companion"[9].

1 Cor 14:1 tells us to "Earnestly desire Spiritual [gifts]". This verse could equally well be translated "earnestly desire the things of the Spirit". It's vitally important that we don't desire spiritual gifts more than the Spirit Himself, or put more emphasis on spiritual gifts than on a relationship

with the Spirit. Developing a close friendship with the Spirit is actually the key to moving in spiritual gifts anyhow. Sadly, we have overemphasised having spiritual gifts and underemphasised knowing the Holy Spirit. He wants our love; he desires our affection.

I believe that the greatest gift of the New Covenant is the Holy Spirit himself. As a student I read JI Packer's book "Knowing God"[10] where he taught that the greatest blessing of New Covenant was adoption into God's family. That is indeed an amazing blessing. But now I've come to see that the greatest blessing is not adoption but the Spirit of adoption. What could be a greater blessing than God Himself living in us? He is the greatest Blessing and the source of all other blessings. The Holy Spirit wants to do us good. He's come as a friend, companion, encourager, Comforter, Counsellor. He's in us to bring righteousness, peace and joy.

The Greek word for "Comforter" comes from *parakaléō* (*pará*, "*from* close-beside" and *kaléō*, "to call") – properly, "make a call" from being "close-up and personal."[11] Holy Spirit has come to be close to us, not someone distant and unknowable. He has come to be close-up and personal because *He is a Person.*

He's deeply in love with us. He is the Lover of our souls. He takes delight in us. He's affectionate; he wants us to feel His love. I remember clearly that is was back in 1994 that I first told the Holy Spirit "I love you Holy Spirit" and then felt a real 'whoosh' in my spirit, as if He was responding with "I love you too". I was deeply touched but at the same time I felt a bit cheated. Why had no one explained all this to me before? Why had no one told me that you could express love to the Holy Spirit and feel love in return? The truth is that He wants to hold us close, to make us feel the Father's love for us. As it says in Rom 5:5, He pours out God's love into our hearts. He enables us to cry from our hearts "Abba", Father" (Rom 8:15).

Yes, at times he brings gentle correction, but never condemnation. Yes, he brings us to repentance but only for the purpose of leading us back to the Father's arms (Luke 15:20). When Satan speaks to us he is harsh and condemning, but the Holy Spirit is gracious and kind (Heb 10:29).

The Holy Spirit comes to make our salvation real to us. Without Him it would be just head knowledge; with Him we can feel it in our hearts. You can't see the wind but you can feel it. Holy Spirit is like the wind - you can't see Him but you can certainly feel Him. He shows us that the good news is not just for everyone but for *me*. Jesus died for *me* (Gal 2:20), the Father loves *me* (1 John 4:10)... The apostle Paul wrote: "Our gospel came to you not simply with words but also with power, with the Holy Spirit and deep conviction." (1 Thess 1:5). "Deep conviction" can be translated "full assurance", "complete confidence" or "entire certainty". The Spirit takes the gospel and makes its truth real in our experience, bringing us full assurance and confidence. He is "the Spirit who clothes faith with certainty"[12].

A few years ago I had a technology upgrade – I bought my first smart phone. Some of you are probably thinking at this moment "not before time!". Well, we think about technology upgrades; why not have an upgrade in your relationship with the Holy Spirit? He wants to take us from one degree of glory to another. I used to think I couldn't get close to the Holy Spirit but I have been finding that He is amazingly affectionate, He's extraordinarily gracious. He wants to take us deeper into a greater experience of God's love and joy.

It may surprise some of you but the Holy Spirit is a fun person to be around. He's full of joy and gladness. He's not here as a kill-joy, but as a joy-giver. He's full of life, he comes to enliven and enlighten. In recent years, I've noticed as a grandfather that when children are happy they smile, but when they are *really* happy they laugh. So it is that the Holy Spirit sometimes fills us with laughter (Ps 126:2). The Spirit brings us a foretaste of future joys (Rom 8:23), and the fruit of a life lived in the Spirit is love, *joy*, peace… (Gal 5:22).

For too long the church has emphasised correct belief without also emphasising correct experience. Holy Spirit comes to make our faith real and to make it personal. It's not just knowing about God, but also experiencing Him. "Now this is eternal life: that they know you, the only true God, and Jesus Christ, whom you have sent" (John 17:3). The word 'know' in the Bible means 'to know by personal encounter'. A love relationship involves feelings and emotions. Furthermore, we have come to share in the "the Holy Spirit's joy" (1 Thess 1:6, NTE), and it's impossible to have joy and not feel it. The Holy Spirit brings us the feelings that belong with our salvation.

## Pursuing

We honour the Holy Spirit by pursuing Him. Pursuing is an active process. Pursuing is not passive; it is not just waiting for the Holy Spirit to come. If we say to the Holy Spirit: "I'm going after you today" He will reply: "That's good, I'm pursuing you also". Then there's going to be a collision, there's going to be an encounter!

We are invited to yield (submit, surrender) to the Holy

Spirit. It is a glad surrender. It is true freedom. The amount the Spirit will work in your life depends on how much you surrender to Him. The Spirit responds to our hunger, our thirst, our desperation. We need an attitude like that of Jacob who said to the angel he was wrestling with "I will not let you go until you bless me" (Gen 32:26). We need the determination of blind Bartimaeus, who, when people told him to stop shouting, he shouted all the louder: "Jesus, Son of David, have mercy on me" (Luke 18:39). We need the persistence of the woman with the issue of blood, who kept pressing through the crowd so she could just touch the hem of Jesus' robe (Luke 8:43-44).

**Fellowship**

Fellowship means a shared life together. Did you know that the Holy Spirit wants to help you in all aspects of life? Did you know that God is interested in the ordinary and mundane? Nothing is too small or insignificant. He's the Helper, He wants to give us a helping hand in everything we do. "In all your ways acknowledge Him (the Holy Spirit)" Prov 3:5-6. He wants to 'do life' with us. For example, Chlo Glassborrow (leader of Catch the Fire London) recounts the story of the Holy Spirit instructed her not to go out for a planned walk with friends but to stay in her flat. Shortly afterwards she heard the noise of water gushing in her home - a huge leak from the washing machine, which she was able to turn off quickly to prevent the whole apartment from being flooded.[13]

Sharing life with the Holy Spirit is also a key to reaching out to others with the good news (Acts 1:8, 8:29, 16:6-7)[14]. And the more people who receive the gospel, the more praise and honour there will be to Jesus (Eph 1:12).

Scripture instructs us "do not quench" (1 Thess 5:19), "do

not grieve" (Eph 4:30), do not resist (Acts 7:51), or insult (Heb 10:29) the Holy Spirit. From these instructions we learn that the Holy Spirit is easily hurt if we fail to respond to Him in the right way. We could therefore add the instruction "do not doubt" - do not doubt his love, his desire for intimacy with us. What most Christians fail to appreciate is that "Intimacy is a goal in itself"[15]. One time the God spoke to Carol Arnott and said "I have many servants but few lovers"[16]. Maybe it's time to re-examine our priorities to make sure we are lovers before workers. And although intimacy with the Holy Spirit is an end in itself, it is also true that "all fruitfulness flows from intimacy", as exemplified by the life of Heidi Baker[17].

Pastor David Diga Hernandez shares four important keys to friendship with Holy Spirit[18]:

1. *Understand* who He is and what He does. Stay in sync with Him. Be receptive, treat Him with honour.

2. *Reverence*. Listen to His voice and don't grieve Him. When He says the word, respect and obey it.

3. *Trust*. Depend on Him, not on ourselves. We need Him in everything. Be led by Him, involving Him in your decisions. Trust Him to speak to you.

4. *Communication*. Ps 139:7-10. He is everywhere. Be aware of Him. Listen for the still, small voice. Think about Him as often as you are able. Slow your pace of life to include Him.

### Worship

Many feel uneasy about worshipping the Spirit. I remember one time when my granddaughter Thea was three years old I made up a song about her and sang it to her. She was really pleased, but then she said "Adam" –

she wanted me to sing a song for her elder brother also. She said this because there was such a close bond between them. The same is true with Holy Spirit and Jesus. If we sing a song of worship to the Spirit, that will please Him, but then He will want us to sing one for Jesus also. There is no cause for concern: He will keep us in balance.

Pastor Mike Shreve gives an amazing list of some things we can praise the Holy Spirit for[19], here are some excerpts:

"Holy Spirit, You are my COMFORTER (John 14:26, KJV);
I would be devastated by the pain of this world without You.

Holy Spirit, You are my HELPER (John 14:26, NKJV);
I would be helpless without You.

Holy Spirit, You are the *PARACLETOS* (the One who stands by; John 14:26);
I would be alone and defenceless without You.

Holy Spirit, You are the WIND of heaven (Acts 2:1-3);
I would succumb to this arid wilderness of sin without You.

Holy Spirit, You are the BREATH OF GOD (Gen. 2:7; John 20:22);
I would die of spiritual asphyxiation without You.

Holy Spirit, You are RIVERS OF LIVING WATER (John 7:38);
My inner being would be a cracked, dry, empty riverbed without You.

Holy Spirit, You are the OIL OF JOY and the OIL OF GLADNESS (Is. 61:3; Ps. 45:7);

I would sink into the depths of depression without Your presence in my heart.

Holy Spirit, You are the SPIRIT OF WISDOM AND UNDERSTANDING (Is. 11:2);
I would make so many foolish choices without You.

Holy Spirit, You are the SPIRIT OF COUNSEL AND MIGHT (Is. 11:2);
I would be oblivious to my purpose and powerless to fulfil it without You.

Holy Spirit, You are the SPIRIT OF ADOPTION (Rom. 8:15);
I would have never become a child of God had You not regenerated my spirit.

Holy Spirit, You are the SPIRIT OF GLORY, THE SHEKINAH (1 Pet. 4:14);
I would have never known the manifest presence of God had You not come.

Holy Spirit, You are the SEAL OF THE LIVING GOD (Eph. 1:13; Rev. 7:2);
I would have surely slipped back into the darkness without Your preserving grip.

Holy Spirit, You are the GUARANTEE OF MY INHERITANCE (Eph. 1:13-14);
I would not have blessed assurance of eternal salvation without Your abiding grace.

Holy Spirit, You are the SPIRIT OF GRACE (Zech. 12:10);
I would have never been recovered from my degraded state had You not rescued me through unearned favor and unmerited love.

Holy Spirit, You are the SPIRIT OF HOPE (Rom 15:13); I would be still lost and without hope had You not revealed Jesus to me."

What can we conclude? Should we worship the Holy Spirit? Yes, with all our heart and soul (Mt 22:37), and with all joy and gladness (Ps 100:2). "Holy Spirit, thank you so much for being in my heart and life today. I yield to You. I surrender to You. I praise You. I celebrate You with all my soul and all my might. I appeal to You to be all that You can be in me today! May I truly fulfil the wondrous calling of being a temple of the Holy Spirit with every precious minute that passes by."[19]

# Honouring the Holy Spirit

## 3 HONOURING THE SPIRIT: THE CORPORATE CONNECTION

How can we honour the Holy Spirit when we meet as a church? We can honour the Holy Spirit in many ways: by loving others, maintaining unity in the church as much as possible, respecting leadership (to give a few examples). Additionally, we honour the Holy Spirit by using spiritual gifts to build up the church and to proclaim the good news. However, in this chapter I want to focus on two questions: How should the pattern of our meetings reflect our devotion to Him, and how should He be worshipped?

**A new pattern**

A few years ago I was leading a cell group and I was thinking about how we can host the Holy Spirit, making Him feel welcome. I then wrote this poem (the first stanza is talking about our grandson Adam, who was 3 years old at the time).

## A Special Someone

Every Wednesday morning a special someone visits our home.
We really look forward to him coming.
We get everything ready –just how he likes it.
We give him a warm welcome and make him feel loved,
We give him a lot of freedom to do as he pleases,
Things get a bit messy at times but it's worth it,
We have fun together.
A lot of love flows between us, and he brings a lot of joy.

Every Thursday evening a special someone visits our Community group
Do we really look forward to Him coming?
Do we prepare ourselves and get things how He likes it?
Do we give Him a warm welcome and make Him feel loved?
Are we ready to give Him the freedom to take over and do as he pleases?
For when He comes things can get a bit messy but it will be worth it,
We will surely have fun together.
A lot of love will flow between us, and He will bring a lot of joy."


The usual pattern of many charismatic church meetings is a time of worship (singing), perhaps with the occasional exercise of spiritual gifts, followed by a time of preaching. But is this pattern biblical? Is this what the Holy Spirit wants? Often this set pattern goes unquestioned and unchallenged.

We have to ask ourselves: why are we substituting our own programs, our own strategies, for the presence of the Holy Spirit? It has been written concerning the Welsh revival: "Had the visitor attended a meeting and asked, 'Who's in charge?' he would have asked in vain. The meetings seemed to have been beyond human control. Not unusually the revivalist, Sidney Evans or Evan Roberts arrived with a singer, some considerable time after the meeting had begun. Spontaneity was the key word. Individual members of the congregation would stand to share a word of encouragement or admonition. Others would lead in prayer. Others would start to sing, whereupon the whole congregation would join in the familiar hymn. There was no order of service, no pre-arranged pattern, no hymnbooks. It just happened, and those present felt that a greater Power was in control."[20] It would perhaps be naïve to think that the Welsh revival presents us with a perfect model, there was a lack of bible-based preaching, for example. Nevertheless, we only have to consider the tremendous blessing that flowed from the revival (including 100,000 conversions in the space of a few months) to see the benefit of allowing the Spirit to blow where He wills, rather than following our own rigid pattern.

It is perhaps informative to see what happened in the early church after the time of the apostles. This was John Wesley's devastating assessment:

"It does not appear that these extraordinary gifts of the Holy Ghost [tongues, prophecies, miracles, etc.] were common in the church for more than two or three centuries. We seldom hear of them after that fatal period when the Emperor Constantine called himself a Christian, and from a vain imagination of promoting the Christian cause thereby heaped riches, and power, and honour, upon the Christians in general; but in particular upon the Christian clergy. From this time they almost totally ceased; very few instances of the kind were found. The cause of this was not (as has been vulgarly supposed,) "because there was no more occasion for them," because all the world was become Christian. This is a miserable mistake; not a twentieth part of it was then nominally Christian. The real cause was, "the love of many," almost of all Christians, so called, was "waxed cold." The Christians had no more of the Spirit of Christ than the other Heathens. The Son of Man, when he came to examine his Church, could hardly "find faith upon earth." This was the real cause why the extraordinary gifts of the Holy Ghost were no longer to be found in the Christian Church — because the Christians were turned Heathens again, and had only a dead form left."[21]

Wesley's critique may be overly harsh, but the truth is that a dynamic relationship with the Holy Spirit was all too quickly replaced by a religious form, where Christianity became about following set rules and beliefs, rather than following the Spirit. Sadly, the church of today has yet to fully recover this loss. Even in the vast majority of charismatic and Pentecostal churches little space is allowed in the Sunday service for the Spirit to move freely. The structure of our meetings often allows little room for the spontaneous moving of the Spirit.

The pattern of meetings of the early church was "When you come together, each of you has a hymn, or a word of instruction, a revelation, a tongue or an interpretation. Everything must be done so that the church may be built up." (1 Cor 14:26). It was a pattern that was meant that the Holy Spirit was allowed free rein; each person present could bring a contribution as and when the Spirit moved them.

We should always be mindful of the Spirit and how we treat Him. We want to make Him feel loved and welcome. We want Him to be happy and feel honoured. We don't just want Him for His gifts; we should just be glad He's with us. It is true that we need both Word and Spirit, but this doesn't mean it's up to us to impose our own structure to keep the two in balance.

Chloe Glassborow says: "My top tip is: if you don't welcome the Holy Spirit, don't expect Him to move. That's the first thing I learnt from Him. It's like [He is saying] 'I am here, but don't just expect me, without welcoming and acknowledging me' "[22]. We should never treat Him casually, or take Him for granted.

## Corporate worship

The Nicene Creed clearly states "We believe in the Holy Spirit, the Lord and Giver of Life, who is worshipped together with the Father and the Son, glorified together with the Father and the Son". Yet in many churches today people feel strangely uncomfortable about worshipping the Holy Spirit. This is simply because most believers have never been taught about doing this. Scripture tells us to worship God (Rev 22:9, Heb 12:28). Since the Holy Spirit is fully God, He should be included in our corporate worship. He is worthy of our praise and adoration. We are commanded: "Love the Lord your God with all your heart, and will all your soul and with all your mind" (Mt 22:37). This command also applies to the Holy Spirit!

For corporate worship, songs directed to the Trinity are a good starting point (e.g. "King of Kings"[23]), but by no means should we be limited to these in our worship of the Spirit. There are a handful of good devotional songs concerning the Holy Spirit but we need more songs that specifically give honour to Him. And let there also be space for spontaneous songs (Eph 5:19).

C.H. Spurgeon makes this assessment: "I am afraid, dear friends, we are too much in the habit of talking of the love of Jesus, without thinking of the love of the Holy Spirit. Now I would not wish to exalt one person of the Trinity above another, but I do feel this, that because Jesus Christ was a man, bone of our bone, and flesh of our flesh, and therefore there was something tangible in him that can be seen with the eyes, and handled with the hands, therefore we more readily think of him, and fix our love on him, than we do upon the Spirit. But why should it be? Let us love Jesus with all our hearts, and let us love the Holy Spirit too. Let us have songs for him, gratitude for him. We do not forget Christ's cross, let us not forget the Spirit's operations. We do not forget what Jesus has done for us, let us always remember what the Spirit does in us. Why you talk of the love, and grace, and tenderness, and faithfulness of Christ, why do you not say the like of the Spirit? Was ever love like his, that he should visit us? Was ever mercy like his, that he should bear with our ill manners, though constantly repeated by us? Was ever faithfulness like his, that multitudes of sins cannot drive him away? Was ever power like his, that overcometh all our iniquities, and yet leads us safely on, though hosts of foes within and without would rob us of our Christian life?

"Oh, the love of the Spirit I sing
By whom is redemption applied."

And unto his name be glory for ever and ever."[24]

# Honouring the Holy Spirit

## 4 HONOURING THE SPIRIT: THE REVIVAL CONNECTION

Honouring the Holy Spirit was the secret of the great revivalists.

**John Wesley**

"Mr. Hall, Kinchin, Ingham, Whitefield, Hatchins, and my brother Charles, were present at our love-feast in Fetter-Lane, with about sixty of our brethren. About three in the morning, as we were continuing constant in prayer, the power of God came mightily upon us, in so much that many cried out for exceeding joy, and many fell to the ground. As soon as we were recovered a little from that awe and amazement at the presence of his Majesty, we broke out with one voice, "We praise thee, O God; we acknowledge thee to be the Lord". This Holy Spirit encounter on Jan 1st 1731 launched John Wesley and his fellow preachers into a new season of revival. His brother reported "Sometimes whole nights were spent in prayer. Often have we been filled as with new wine. And often have we [been] overwhelmed with the divine presence and crying out, 'Will God indeed dwell with men upon earth? ...This is none other than the house of God and the gate of heaven'"[25]. Wesley preached the necessity of honouring the work of the Spirit in all aspects of the Christian life.

## Richard Radcliffe

Richard Radcliffe was greatly used by God in the 1859-1862 revival (sometimes known as the second evangelical awakening). "A follower of his noted that in open air services he would go around the circled assembly, while one was addressing the crowd, his eye filled with anxiety and his lips trembling with emotion, as he whispered to believers as he passed them "brethren, pray for the power of the Holy Spirit on the people." His follower believed that the reason for Radcliffe's success as an evangelist and soul winner was due to the special honour that he put upon the Divine Spirit, giving Him His place in the application of the redemption work of Jesus Christ."[26]

## DL Moody

After several years of intense striving, when he was near to burnout, Moody became convinced of his need of the Holy Spirit. Following a powerful "baptism in the Holy Spirit" he became even more effective as an evangelist, preaching sometimes to crowds of tens of thousands, speaking with great power and authority and with increasing effectiveness in terms of people finding Christ. The striving that had marked his early days was gone as he trusted the Holy Spirit to work through him. He emphasized the Holy Spirit in all his teaching from this time on: "We all need it [the filling of the Holy Spirit] together, and let us not rest day nor night until we possess it; if that is the uppermost thought in our hearts, God will give it to us if we just hunger and thirst for it and say, 'God helping me, I will not rest until endued with power from on high.'"[27]

## Evan Roberts

During the Welsh Revival in 1904 the new converts were instructed by Evan Roberts to pray four things:

1. Send the Spirit now, for Jesus Christ's sake.
2. Send the Spirit powerfully now, for Jesus Christ's sake.
3. Send the Spirit more powerfully now, for Jesus Christ's sake.
4. Send the Spirit still more powerfully now, for Jesus Christ's sake.[28]

And he gave these instructions:

"1. Confess all known sin.
2. Deal with and get rid of anything 'doubtful' in one's life.
3. Be ready to obey the Holy Spirit instantly.
4. Confess Christ publicly.
These are the four things leading to the grand blessing [of revival]."
Roberts especially emphasised step 3: complete and immediate obedience to the Holy Spirit. "Say not 'something prompts me to pray', it is not something it is the Holy Ghost. Whatsoever He says to you, do it! The world may laugh, He did not; you will not be here long. Bow to Him now. Do not say 'hush' when one breaks into prayer. Resist not the Spirit."[29]

Roberts gave special place to the Holy Spirit and emphasised complete and entire surrender to the Spirit as the key to both personal renewal and national revival.

## A revival for today?

If you read the history of revivals it is clear that some places have experienced many waves of revival. Wales was known as "The land of revivals", and the Outer Hebrides had seen many recent outpourings of the Spirit before the well-known 1949-52 revival. Surely the people in these places knew what it was to pursue God wholeheartedly, and to have an expectation that there would be a new visitation of the Holy Spirit. There has to be a holy desperation to see revival, including seeking Him with tears.[30] We can talk a lot about praying for revival. But all revival must include personal revival. That's why we should first pray "Lord, send a revival and let it begin with me".

I have been a Christian for over 40 years, and in my experience the high water mark for the working of the Spirit in the UK churches was in the mid-90s, popularly known as "The Toronto Blessing". Many were surprised and delighted at what God did[31,32,33]. Since that time there has generally been a widespread decline in the work of the Spirit. Sadly, most people don't seem be too bothered about this situation. I especially am concerned that the younger generation will think "This is all there is" when the truth is much different. The reasons for this decline are manifold, but foremost I see that we have failed to pursue, honour and love the Holy Spirit. We may still pray "Welcome Holy Spirit" but in practice we mean "Welcome, but don't interfere with our timetable too much". Far too many churches are resisting the Holy Spirit (Acts 7:51).

The truth is that we can't have church as usual when the Spirit moves. It disturbs the status quo; it rocks the boat.

This disruption is not welcomed by everyone (especially the religious). As someone observed in 1994: "Some people don't like the boat being rocked, even when it's God doing the rocking". It's like opening the window on a hot day. At first it's a refreshing breeze. But then the wind gets stronger, it starts blowing papers about. Now it is getting a bit uncomfortable, a bit untidy, a bit messy, a bit 'out of control'. Many would say "Time to shut the window again"; in other words it's time to 'get back to normal'. I say "No, it's time to open the window wider!". And when you've genuinely encountered the Holy Spirit, there is no going back, you are forever changed. You can't settle for 'church as usual'. But for some that's controversial, it creates tension. Some want to stick with the 'status quo', while others want to move forwards. To avoid causing division some have sought to 'shut things down'. The result has been that the supernatural is draining away from the churches of today. It can be messy, it can be inconvenient, it can be costly when the Spirit moves, but it is so worth it. We owe it to the Church and the world to have the Spirit move dynamically among us, so that everyone might see a demonstration of Jesus' life and power[34] (1 Cor 2:4).

It feels appropriate to let my friend C.H. Spurgeon have the final word on the subject:

"Until our churches honor the Holy Spirit, we shall never see [Him] abundantly manifested in our midst. Let the preacher always confess before he preaches that he relies upon the Holy Spirit. Let him burn his manuscript and depend upon the Holy Spirit. If the Spirit does not come to help him, let him be still and let the people go home and pray that the Spirit will help him the next service... We must honor the Spirit; unless we put Him first, He will never make crowns for us to wear. He will get victories, but He will have the honor of them, and if we do not give to Him the honor, He will never give to us the privilege and success. And best of all, if you would have the Holy Spirit, let us meet together earnestly to pray for Him. Remember, the Holy Spirit will not come to us as a church, unless we seek Him...

Now, it is the work of the Holy Spirit that I wish to especially direct to your attention, and I may as well mention the reason why I do. It is this: in the United States of America, there has been a great awakening... Now, to have a similar effect produced in this land, the one thing we must seek is the outpouring of the Holy Spirit. I thought that perhaps my writing about the work of the Holy Spirit might fulfil the text, "Them that honour me I will honour" (1 Sam 2:30). My sincere desire is to honor the Holy Spirit, and if He will be pleased to honor His church in return, unto Him shall be the glory forever."[35]

# Honouring the Holy Spirit

## ENDNOTES

[1] "Honoring the Holy Spirit as God" John Van Gelderen. https://www.revivalfocus.org/honoring-holy-spirit-god/
[2] "Early Christian Writings", *Trans* Maxwell Staniforth, p.130, Penguin Books Ltd, London, 1968. Polycarp's prayer was likely based on an even earlier Eucharistic prayer.
[3] If I should be accused of teaching heresy then at least I will be in very good company.
[4] https://effectualgrace.com/2019/08/02/charles-spurgeon-on-words-from-the-lord/
[5] https://archive.spurgeon.org/sermons/0315.php
[6] Wesley's notes on the Bible. https://www.christianity.com/bible/commentary.php?com=wes&b=45&c=8
[7] Gordon Fee, quoted in "God's Lavish Grace" Terry Virgo 2004, p.134, Monarch Books
[8] "The Holy Spirit: Unbounded Gift of Joy" Mary Ann Fatula, Michael Glazier books, 1998
[9] "Soaking in the Spirit" Carol Arnott, Destiny Image Publishers Inc, 2020
[10] "Knowing God" JI Packer, Hodder and Staughton, 1973
[11] https://biblehub.com/greek/3870.htm
[12] "See What a Morning (Resurrection hymn)" Stuart Townend & Keith Getty Copyright © 2003 Thankyou Music
[13] Chlo Glassborow "I believe" TBN UK broadcast August 2021
[14] "Solid Foundations: An Introductory Course for new Christians" Paul Mould, Kindle Edition, 2021. In this e-book I recount (p. 18-20) an example of how the Spirit led me in sharing the good news.
[15] "Living in the Father's love" Marj Rossol, Manchester Vinelife Podcast 2014
[16] "Soaking in the Spirit" p. 88
[17] "Soaking in the Spirit" p. 11

[18] https://www.bibliatodo.com/En/online-sermons/how-to-become-a-friend-of-the-holy-spirit-4-keys-david-diga-hernandez/ (posted 2019)
[19] https://www.charismanews.com/opinion/46055-expressing-worship-to-the-holy-spirit Copyright © 2013 Mike Shreve (adapted)
[20] https://www.methodistevangelicals.org.uk/Articles/523349/The_Welsh_Revival.aspx
[21] "The More Excellent Way" John Wesley, cited in https://peopleneedjesus.net/2017/05/30/seven-ways-john-wesley-preached-about-the-holy-spirit/
[22] Catch the Fire London, Facebook live, June 2020
[23] "King of Kings" Geoff Bullock 2019 © So Essential Tunes, Shout! Music Publishing, Hillsong Music Publishing Australia
[24] C.H. Spurgeon https://www.blueletterbible.org/Comm/spurgeon_charles/sermons/0278.cfm
[25] https://lexloiz.wordpress.com/2009/08/14/a-prayer-meeting-that-changed-the-world/
[26] https://www.1859.org.uk/the-people-god-used/reginald-radcliffe
[27] Felicity Dale https://simplychurch.com/2012/07/18/the-holy-spirit-and-dl-moody/
[28] "Carriers of the Fire", p44, Karen Lowe, Shedhead Productions, Llanelli, 2004
[29] https://www.sermonindex.net/modules/newbb/viewtopic.php?topic_id=2042&forum=40 (posted 2004)
[30] "It's Happening: A Generation is Crying Out, and Heaven is Responding" William McDowell, Charisma House, 2018
[31] "Catch the Fire: The Toronto Blessing : an Experience of Renewal and Revival" Guy Chevreau, HarperCollins, 1995
[32] "The Father's blessing" John Arnott, Creation House, 1995
[33] Some people were critical of the physical manifestations of the Holy Spirit such as shaking, laughter and shouting, but these effects were common in past revivals. See e.g. "Carriers of the Fire" p 153.
[34] I love John Arnott's passion about this: "I am at the point where I say 'God, come and blow our doors off. Lord, just come, let your presence come, let it come, let it come. I welcome you'. I cannot tolerate the way the church has been losing ground year after year". "The Father's blessing" p. 143

[35] https://www.revivalfocus.org/spurgeon-honoring-holy-spirit/. Revival began in the UK a few months after Spurgeon preached this sermon in 1858.

# Honouring the Holy Spirit

### BIBLE QUOTATIONS

Unless otherwise indicated, all Scripture quotations are taken from The Holy Bible, New International Version® NIV® Copyright © 1973 1978 1984 2011 by Biblica, Inc. TM. Used by permission. All rights reserved worldwide. www.zondervan.com. The "NIV" and "New International Version" are trademarks registered in the United States Patent and Trademark Office by Biblica, Inc.®

Scripture quotations marked "KJV" are from The Authorized (King James) Version. Rights in the Authorized Version in the United Kingdom are vested in the Crown. Reproduced by permission of the Crown's patentee, Cambridge University Press.

Scripture quotations marked "NLT" are taken from New Living Translation, copyright ©1996, 2004, 2015 by Tyndale House Foundation. Used by permission of Tyndale House Publishers, Carol Stream, Illinois 60188. All rights reserved.

Quotations designated (NET) are from the NET Bible® copyright ©1996, 2019 by Biblical Studies Press, L.L.C. http://netbible.com All rights reserved.

# Honouring the Holy Spirit

## ABOUT THE AUTHOR

Paul was born in Leicestershire, England, but has spent almost all his adult life in the Manchester area. He formerly worked as a Biochemist, Cell Biologist, and Biophysicist at the University of Manchester, UK. Following his recent retirement he has acted as a Trustee of a local Foodbank, led a bible study for refugees, and taken up his enthusiasm for Christian writing. This is his third book, which he considers as his most important to date. Paul's real passion is the Person and work of the Holy Spirit.

Also published as: *Mould, Paul. Honouring the Holy Spirit. Kindle Edition.*

Printed in Great Britain
by Amazon